C000177516

**BERLIN
IN FIFTY
DESIGN ICONS**

# 50

the
**DESIGN
MUSEUM**

BERLIN
**IN FIFTY
DESIGN ICONS**

SOPHIE
LOVELL

50

conran
OCTOPUS

# BERLIN

# INTRODUCTION

Perhaps the most fascinating thing about Berlin is that it is a major European capital that is still defining itself. Berlin's modern history has been so often interrupted in such radical ways that the city remains in a continual state of transformation: always becoming, never quite being – not yet, anyway.

Berlin has been able to change so much because it still has the space to do so. Today's population of 3.5 million has not yet reached the level of the 1920s and 1930s, when it was over 4 million. Many of the gaps left by both war and Wall were vacant for a long time, to be informally occupied by anyone who had the inclination to do so, from the communal gardening projects at the former Tempelhof airfield to the clubs and bars housed in former industrial buildings all over the city. Commerce is catching up, however: people flock to Berlin to enjoy exactly this alternative 'urban commons' experience, but the spaces are now slowly being filled by giant retail constructions and 'luxury' housing.

In terms of architecture, Berlin is distinctive in its 'onion skin' aspect – all layers of its history visible at once, revealing, not hiding. Although there are some real neoclassical gems, on the Museumsinsel (Museum Island) for example, it is the International Style, postwar approaches built under two ideologies, picking up on modernism, the Werkbund and the Bauhaus, that are the main icons here.

There is a distinct lack of post-reunification starchitecture in Berlin, and one cannot help but feel that opportunities for defining a genuinely contemporary architectural language were missed, with Potsdamer Platz being a prime example. Instead, it is the quiet reminders of things never to be forgotten and the initiatives of the populace, both old and new, that have created the current zeitgeist of the city: a snapshot of now in what is once again, after almost a century, a city with a heady atmosphere of hedonism and an 'anything goes' attitude.

Berlin's unique history is written all over its face, from bullet-scarred façades to East and West versions of 20th century development. It is precisely the way the city has embraced its past – both good and, at times, unspeakably bad – that makes it so fascinating.

# BRANDENBURG GATE QUADRIGA

The turbulent life of one of Berlin's most famous ladies

There is a popular myth in Berlin that the Quadriga, the sculpture of a chariot drawn by four horses atop the iconic Brandenburg Gate, once faced westward rather than east, as it does now, and had its orientation changed at various points in the city's troubled history. Like all good myths, this is entirely untrue but, nevertheless, typical for Berlin, the Quadriga has had quite a topsy-turvy history.

The copper sculpture, which originally depicted the goddess of peace Eirene in a horse-drawn chariot, was designed by Johann Gottfried Schadow (1764–1850) in 1793 when the classicist Brandenburger Tor really did function as a gate in the city wall. Fewer than 20 years later, the sculpture was carried off to Paris as booty by Napoleon when he defeated the Prussians in 1806, only to be triumphantly recovered and restored to its place eight years later when the charioteer was apparently altered to represent Victoria, goddess of victory, instead. All but destroyed during the Second World War, the sculpture was reconstructed by the East German government (in collaboration with the West German government, who had kept a plaster cast of the original). Damaged by New Year's Eve revellers in 1990, the Quadriga was restored once again and returned to its position in August 1991 – facing east, as it has always done.

One of the best-known landmarks in Germany, the Brandenburg Gate is one of those places where history was made. It was here in 1987 that Ronald Reagan declared, 'Mr Gorbachev, open this gate. Mr Gorbachev, tear down this wall!' And two years later images of East German citizens pouring through this same gate were broadcast around the world as the Wall fell and Germany's reunification began.

For a statue, Eirene is a much-travelled dame. In 1958, she was unseated yet again from her post, this time for restoration.

# KARL FRIEDRICH SCHINKEL
Berlin's Baumeister

The architect Karl Friedrich Schinkel (1781–1841) began the transformation of Berlin from unspectacular provincial city to great European capital with the construction of a series of exceptional buildings that established the city at the forefront of architectural experimentation.

After studying architecture, Schinkel first made his name as a painter and set designer, working on operas and the painted panoramas popular then. In 1815, the first of a series of state appointments as Privy Building Officer meant his new stage set became Berlin itself, and his designs are today symbols of city and state: from the spectacular severe-columned portico of the Altes Museum (1823–30) to the design for the original Iron Cross medal.

Schinkel continued experimenting with style and material, producing neogothic structures and buildings in cast iron – The Prussian National Monument for the Liberation Wars in Kreuzberg (1818–26) – and soaring brick – the Friedrichswerder Church in Mitte (1824–31).

Most radical was his Bauakademie building (1832–36), which abandoned historicist references, anticipating modernism in its stripped grid-like façades. Demolished in 1962 after war damage, today it has been recreated at a 1:1 scale: its façades printed on fabric over a scaffold structure – with plans afoot to rebuild it in honour of Schinkel's genius.

Completed in 1818, Schinkel's neoclassical Neue Wache (New Guardhouse) on Unter den Linden originally served as part of the Royal Palace. It is now the Central Memorial of the Federal Republic of Germany for the Victims of War and Dictatorship, and houses a bronze sculpture of a woman cradling her fallen son by Käthe Kollwitz (1867–1945), who lost her youngest son in the First World War and was persecuted by the Nazis during the Second World War.

# BERLIN STREETLIGHTS
## The city in light years

Look a little closer if you fly into Berlin at night and you'll notice that all that glistens is not uniform; the city from above emits light in two distinct hues: orange light coming from the sodium-vapour lamps in the east, while a softer, greenish light is produced by their gas-lamp cousins in the west.

While exploring Berlin it pays to look up and notice the details. The capital's varied streetlamp styles can tell you a lot about which part of the city you are in and all its historical overlaps.

The view is just as interesting on the ground, as there is an incredible range of lamp-post designs in the city: lighting the way down Karl-Marx-Allee, for example, are 215 double-headed lamps designed in the early 1950s by German Democratic Republic (GDR) architect Richard Paulick (1903–79), who had previously worked at the Bauhaus in Dessau. On Straße des 17. Juni, you'll find one of the last remaining elements of the Nazi state's Germania vision in the form of streetlights designed by one Albert Speer (1905–81). In stark contrast, just up the road are the lamps architects Axel Schultes (b. 1943) and Charlotte Frank (b. 1959) designed to match their new Federal Chancellery building, completed in 2001.

The first gas lamps were installed in Berlin on Unter den Linden in 1826 and, even today, half the world's existing gas streetlights, some 36,000 of them, are found in Berlin. Many are historical cast-iron designs – there is a nice little open-air museum of them (Gaslaternen-Freilichtmuseum) in the Tiergarten near the S-Bahn (city railway) station. Plans are afoot to replace all the gas lamps with more energy-efficient LED lighting, but these have hit a budget-induced stalemate, so residents of west Berlin will be able to enjoy their city by gaslight for some years to come.

# THE GOLDEN ANGEL
Winged victory or something else?

At the hub of the Großer Stern (Great Star) roundabout, the point at which the boulevards that criss-cross Tiergarten meet, is the Siegessäule or Victory Column. A major Berlin landmark, it was commissioned following Prussia's defeat of Denmark in 1864 but, by the time it was completed, the Prussian army had been so victoriously prolific that the 69-metre- (226-foot) high column came to be adorned with a total of three rings of captured cannons to mark the Austro–Prussian War of 1866 and Franco–Prussian War of 1871 as well. Inaugurated in 1873, the column is crowned with a gilded bronze sculpture by Friedrich Drake (1805–82) of the goddess Victoria. It initially stood in front of the Reichstag and was moved to its current location in 1938 as part of Albert Speer's Germania plan. A fourth ring was added above the cannons on Hitler's direct order (he wanted it to be bigger!), made up not of cannons but garlands.

Most Berliners know the gleaming winged figure simply as *Goldelse* (Gold Elsa), after the 1866 book of the same name by German novelist E. Marlitt. And, despite its military origins, film fans associate *Else* with something completely different: as a resting spot for two angels who call the skies above Berlin home, in Wim Wenders' haunting 1987 portrait of the still-divided city, *Der Himmel Über Berlin* (released in English as *Wings of Desire*).

*Goldelse*'s non-military credentials were enhanced further when during the 1990s her figure became the emblem of the annual Love Parade, a techno music festival whose crowds of up to 1.5 million ravers congregated around the base of the column. During his 2008 campaign, President-to-be Barack Obama also held his famous speech here to an audience of over 200,000.

The goddess Victoria does not so much represent victory in war as victory over adversity and death; perhaps that's why Berliners have such a soft spot for their golden angel. *Goldelse* appears as a motif throughout Wim Wenders' *Wings of Desire*. At one point one of the two angel protagonists surveys the panoramic view of the city from the top of the column while the voice of a recently visited human who has just cheated death recites a list of small earthly pleasures – 'the peaceful Sunday, riding a bicycle with no hands' – and as he turns from looking west towards the then walled-off east, 'the beautiful stranger'.

# POTSDAMER PLATZ TRAFFIC LIGHT
The first of its kind

'Potsdamer Platz looks like a suppurating wound', wrote journalist and novelist Joseph Roth (1894–1939) in 1924 of the major traffic intersection at the heart of the city. Back then, it was one of the busiest in Europe and that same year it became the site of the continent's first-ever set of traffic lights, developed by Siemens and designed by Peter Behrens' studio chief, Jean Krämer (1886–1943). Roth's words gained added poignance when Potsdamer Platz, once the physical manifestation of the frenetic pace of the city as 'Electropolis', was left utterly decimated by the war, a void that was the widest point of the Berlin Wall's 'death strip'. The site was immortalized in Wim Wenders' classic film *Wings of Desire* where an old man mournfully walks through the wasteland, muttering in despair that he 'cannot find the Potsdamer Platz'.

The traffic returned in the 1990s, when the 'wound' became a European record breaker once more – this time as Europe's biggest building site. The redeveloped Potsdamer Platz includes buildings by Renzo Piano (b. 1937), Richard Rogers (b. 1933), Hans Kollhoff (b. 1946) and Helmut Jahn (b. 1940). At its centre, duly reinstated alongside more modern brethren in 1997, is a replica of the Siemens 1924 'traffic light tower', resplendent with a clock face plus a glass-windowed room for a lone police officer to preside over vehicular proceedings below and take in the vista above – a rare sight in Berlin – of towering skyscrapers.

There is not a single feature remaining from the Potsdamer Platz of the 1920s that is recognizable on this site today – except for the replica of the square's original traffic light masquerading as a clock. At a height of 8.5 metres (28 feet), this structure is now dwarfed by the surrounding high-rises, which include Renzo Piano's Daimler Building and Helmut Jahn's Sony Center.

# AEG TURBINE HALL
A classic temple of modern industry

In 1907 Peter Behrens (1868–1940), one of Germany's very first industrial designers, became the leading artistic consultant for the Allgemeine Elektrizitäts-Gesellschaft (General Electricity Company), a manufacturer of electrical equipment better known by its initials – AEG. His responsibility was to develop all aspects of the company's public appearance starting with their logo, through all the products and even the factories – including this new turbine production hall in Huttenstraße 12–19 in the Moabit district. With his tight control of AEG's company aesthetics, Peter Behrens pretty much defined the idea of what we now know as corporate identity.

With the completion of the Turbine Hall, which is 123 metres (404 feet) long and stands 25 metres (82 feet) high, in 1909, Behrens also set the stage for a new industrial architecture in Berlin and beyond. Although he still incorporated classical elements, such as Egyptianesque corner towers, and retained a resemblance to Greek classical proportions in the rhythm of the façade, the building represents a complete style change towards a new, modern, stripped-down form incorporating a blend of brick, glass and steel.

The perfection with which this century-old building combines form and function is perhaps best evinced by the fact that it continues to fulfil its original function: the assembly of power turbines, only now they are state-of-the-art gas ones instead.

The 1909 AEG Turbine Hall in Moabit, designed by Peter Behrens, is perhaps the biggest 20th century design icon in this book, and for all sorts of reasons.

# BERLIN KEY
## Behind closed doors

An absolute tongue twister of a German word, *Durchsteck-schlüssel* translates into English as 'push-through key' but this intriguing object, which looks like something straight out of a René Magritte painting, is more commonly known simply as the Berlin Key. It is an ingenious solution to a problem affecting the classic 19th-century *Mietskaserne* (rental barracks), Berlin tenement blocks, arranged as a series of courtyards backing onto one another, accessible through various communal doors. Residents were encouraged to ensure they locked up behind themselves at night but many would forget.

It was Johannes Schweiger, a locksmith for the Berlin-based Albert Kerfin & Co. who proposed the system. The 'double-bearded' key is inserted into an upside-down U-shaped lock, which, once turned to unlock the door from the outside, can then only be retrieved by pushing it through to the interior side of the door and turning it again from that side – this time locking the door. Schweiger's employers mass-produced the system from 1912 onwards and, although more advanced measures have since taken over, many doors are still opened and closed this way on account of preservation orders.

Given the Berlin Key's surreal appearance, it's perhaps little wonder that French sociologist Bruno Latour (b. 1947) chose to entitle a 1991 essay on the power of objects to compel people to act according to social contrasts, 'The Berlin key or how to do words with things', which fits well with the German knack of doing things with words.

At the end of the 19th century Berlin was in the throes of an industrial boom and that meant a dramatic increase in workers in the city who all needed housing. Many new tenement blocks were built and communal key solutions for the main entrances became a necessity – one of which was the Berlin Key.

# HUFEISENSIEDLUNG
## Horseshoe housing for the masses

Like those of many of the major metropolises across Europe, Berlin's population swelled in the early 20th century. Rapid industrialization drew Germans out of the countryside and into the cities, pushing the housing capacities of Berlin's peripheral neighbourhoods – such as Kreuzberg and Prenzlauer Berg – to breaking point.

In response to the need for new homes, a non-profit building society and housing cooperative was set up in 1924 and soon commissioned architects to create progressive housing for Berlin's working class. Among them was Bruno Taut (1880–1938), whose Hufeisensiedlung (Horseshoe Estate) in Neukölln remains one of the finest examples of modernist housing in Europe.

Taut was a committed socialist, and his distinctive horseshoe-shaped estate revels in the ideals of modernity and the future. With its monolithic curved mass, flat roofs and tastefully simple interiors, the Hufeisensiedlung provided light and comfortable homes for 3,000 Berliners in contrast to the often overcrowded and insanitary conditions of many of the old neighbourhoods.

Yet the real gem of the estate is colour, which Taut saw as a vital tool to be used in architecture, especially when budgets were limited. Through contrasting patterns and hues the Hufeisensiedlung assumes a varied and surprising personality that is often lacking in the homogenous housing estates of later years.

Thanks to massive population growth, Berlin is currently once again suffering from a severe housing shortage. It may be nearly a hundred years old but there is still much to learn from Bruno Taut's 1925–1933 mass-housing model.

# KPM URBINO
Trude Petri's definitive dinner service

Unlike some European capital cities such as Vienna, Berlin has relatively few manufacturers or family firms still in operation. It is not easy to find examples of locally produced goods that have endured, especially in such a beleaguered industry as domestic porcelain. The Königliche Porzellan-Manufaktur Berlin (Royal Porcelain Factory), or KPM for short, is therefore a bit of an exception. Founded in 1763 by Friedrich the Great, the company still operates from its (admittedly new) premises on the edge of the Tiergarten.

KPM made its name with 18th-century Rococco designs, but it is the designs from the early 20th century that are the most popular today – in particular, a simple white service called Urbino, designed in 1929 by a young ceramicist called Trude Petri (1906–98), which was awarded the Grand Prix at the Paris International Exposition in 1937.

Petri studied in Hamburg before moving to Berlin to finish her training and start work at KPM in 1927. The design that made her name, officially launched in 1931, is a superb example of the Neue Sachlichkeit (New Objectivity) movement which had just begun to influence the company through the Deutscher Werkbund and the Bauhaus. Urbino is a functional design that nevertheless exhibits an air of almost whimsical delicacy, notably in the finely curved handles of the cups and teapot. It remains to this day one of KPM's biggest-selling designs.

Trude Petri's Urbino design was influenced, not just by the ideas of the Bauhaus and Werkbund, but also by a large exhibition of Chinese ceramics that was showing in Berlin at the Akademie der Künste at the time.

# MUSEUM ISLAND
Berlin's beating cultural heart

The Museumsinsel (Museum Island), in the Spree River in the middle of the city, has been a work in progress since its first building, the Altes Museum (Old Museum) designed by Karl Friedrich Schinkel (see page 10), was completed here in 1830. With the opening of the Pergamon Museum a century later in 1930, Berlin was able to boast a unique ensemble of five world-renowned museums containing art and artefact collections ranging from ancient civilizations to the 19th century. The most famous residents here are the bust of Queen Nefertiti in the Neues Museum, and the Ishtar Gate in the Pergamon. The museum buildings, in their various classical styles, can be seen as a celebration of the self-confidence of the rising bourgeoisie and the idea of making culture and art accessible to the public.

The Museum Island was heavily damaged during the Second World War and although the Pergamon Museum and the Altes Museum were renovated during GDR times, the Neues Museum remained a ruin until the 1990s when British architect David Chipperfield (b. 1953) was selected to restore it. In 1999, the same year that the Museum Island was named a UNESCO World Heritage Site, a masterplan was approved to turn the island into a Louvre on the Spree. The scheme won't be completed until the 2020s but, when finished, all five museums will be accessible through one final new building, the James Simon Galerie, also designed by David Chipperfield Architects.

Designed by Friedrich August Stüler and Johan Heinrich Strack, the late classical/neorenaissance Alte Nationalgalerie (Old National Gallery) of 1876 is one of the most beautiful and imposing buildings on the Museum Island, now a UNESCO World Heritage Site.

# ALEXANDERPLATZ UNDERGROUND STATION
A sea of green beneath the chaos

Berlin Alexanderplatz would be unrecognizable today to the first readers of Alfred Döblin's eponymous novel of 1929. It is a chaotic nightmare to navigate: an obstacle course of lost tourists, *Currywurst* vendors, buskers and impromptu commercial structures in the shadow of the Fernsehturm (TV Tower) and an eclectic mix of architecture more bad than good. Yet, descend into the subterranean realms of the public transport system and a pleasant surprise awaits in the form of Alexanderplatz U-Bahnhof, designed by Alfred Grenander (1863–1931).

The Swedish architect was Berlin's most prominent station builder from the first years of the 20th century up until his death in 1931, during which time he designed underground stations across the city in styles ranging from the neoclassicism of Wittenbergplatz to the modernism of Krumme Lanke.

At Alexanderplatz, signature Grenander details abound, such as riveted steel columns supporting high ceilings and hemispheric lamps illuminating the large platform areas. But most captivating are the glazed green tiles, another signature of Grenander's, who used colour to allow passengers to instantly identify the stations they pass through. With subtle variations in colour between mint and chartreuse, it's easy to while away the minutes gazing into the green and enjoying the respite from the melee above.

Besides Alexanderplatz, Alfred Grenander was also responsible for the design of a large number of other U-Bahn stations in the 1920s, including Wittenbergplatz, Hermannplatz, parts of Nollendorfplatz, Krumme Lanke and the wonderfully named Onkel-Toms-Hütte (Uncle Tom's Cabin), as well as stations along the U8 line, including Rosenthaler Platz and Jannowitzbrücke.

# THE SHELL BUILDING
Go with the flow

How do you give movement to a static form? The Shell-Haus (Shell Building) is a German masterpiece of classic modernism. Designed by Emil Fahrenkamp (1885–1966), it opened in 1932 and was immediately hailed as an iconic work of truly modern construction. Fahrenkamp was searching for new ways to utilize the technological innovations of his time and, as a result, the Shell-Haus was not only one of the first high-rises with a steel frame construction but also featured ribbons of windows to create light and transparent offices. Organized in four wings around an inner courtyard, all floors and offices are filled with natural light, which was nothing less than a sensation at that time.

Yet the building is also a bit of a bastard, in terms of not being truly modern throughout. It sticks with some pre-modern traditions in that there are no open-floor plans inside but single, separate rooms, and it's dynamically rounded façade is clad in a very trad Roman travertine.

The graceful curves of the façade are of course the most striking feature. Reminiscent of the flow of the adjacent Landwehr canal, the house moves forward in six gentle waves while also increasing in height from six to ten levels along. Underlining this continuous fluid façade, the windows and stone panels are curved, too. It is still used as office space today, not as a headquarters for the Shell Oil Company, but for Berlin's main gas firm instead.

Ruffled like a scallop shell, the Shell-Haus was Emil Fahrenkamp's masterpiece. One of Germany's most noted architects in the 1920s, he continued to work during the Nazi period (his portfolio included the redesign of a castle as a guest house for Joseph Goebbels and the Herman Göring Master School for Painting) and, surprisingly, he maintained an active post-war career until his death in the 1960s.

# OLYMPIC STADIUM
From Hitler to Hertha

A short trip on the S5 S-Bahn from the city centre will take you out to the site of the infamous 1936 Olympic Games – the ones at which American athlete Jesse Owens famously ran all over the myth of Aryan supremacy and scuppered the Nazi PR campaign by claiming four gold medals. This huge anti-modernist architectural complex, designed by Werner March (1894–1976), includes several stadiums and a stunning swimming pool, which is still in use, but the main feature is the elliptical former athletics stadium, built to seat 110,000 people. Intended as a coliseum for the Third Reich, this most Nazi-looking of Nazi buildings was immortalized in Leni Riefenstahl's 1938 propaganda film *Olympia*.

In 1963 the Olympic Stadium became home to the Berlin football team Hertha BSC and in 2000–2004 it was renovated by architects Gerkan, Marg und Partner, who added a new roof and reduced the seating to 74,500, although it remains Germany's largest-seating-capacity stadium.

On your way back to the station it is worth balancing out the anti-modernism with Le Corbusier's striking 1957 modernist Wohnmaschine next door: one of the architect's five Unités d'Habitation in Europe. Although this one Le Corbusier (1887–1965) disowned because the German housing regulators demanded adaptations to his design that he felt spoiled the proportions.

Werner March's 1936 Olympic stadium in Berlin was completely renovated to meet UEFA category 4 stadium requirements in time for the 2006 World Cup hosted by Germany. It is one of many examples of architecture in Berlin that has been reappropriated from the past – but without denying or trying to hide its history.

# SOVIET MEMORIAL IN TREPTOWER PARK
The mighty and the fallen

There are many memorials in Berlin, a city whose people have had more than their fair share of horrors and suffering. Some of them are very quiet and excruciatingly touching, such as Käthe Kollwitz's Unknown Soldier in the Neue Wache, or the memorial to the Nazi book-burning on Bebel Platz, and there are others who try to abstractly address the unspeakable, like the 2,700 blank concrete stelae of Peter Eisenmann's Holocaust Memorial.

In Treptower Park lies one of the city's most remarkable commemorative public spaces that is simultaneously a massive statement of national power. This is the last resting place of more than 5,000 Red Army soldiers who fell during the Battle for Berlin in the last weeks of the Second World War, and a memorial to all the Soviet troops who perished. The Soviet Memorial's 100,000-square-metre (108,000-square-foot) site of solid granite packs a massive punch. It is both awe-inspiring and deeply unsettling. Heading through the entrance gate at the north of the site, one first encounters a statue of a grieving female figure clutching her chest, representing the Motherland weeping for her fallen sons. Beyond her a striking panorama of the war cemetery opens up, framed by two huge draped Soviet flags fashioned from some of that red granite. Though his image is conspicuous by its absence, the voice of Stalin echoes down the sides of the main square, in the form of quotations (Russian on the left, German on the right) emblazoned on the 16 sarcophagi that line it.

The *pièce de résistance* in this striking statement of powerplay lies at the far end of the long sweep of the site: fashioned by Soviet sculptor Yevgeny Vuchetich (1908–74) and standing 11 metres (36 feet) high atop a Russian-style kurgan (burial mound) is a soldier with sword in one hand, rescued child in another, and – just to drive the point home – a crushed swastika underfoot.

# KARL-MARX-ALLEE (FORMER STALINALLEE)

'Europe's last great true street'

Few streets in the world inspire awe quite like Karl-Marx-Allee. Originally named Stalinallee upon its completion in the early 1950s, this valley of monumental communist urbanism forms the beginning of a great axis leading from Alexanderplatz towards Moscow and was designed as a manifestation of the values of the new GDR state: centralization, hierarchy and monumentality.

The boulevard is populated with large residential buildings containing some of the most consistently sought-after apartments in east Berlin, originally primarily reserved for distinguished GDR party members. The eight-storey buildings are renowned for their 'wedding-cake' (*Zuckerbäckerstil*) architecture, combining the neoclassicism of Karl Friedrich Schinkel (see page 10) and the rectilinear formality of the Soviet Union punctuated with ceramic tiles from Meissen in Saxony. Bookending the residential blocks are dual towers designed by GDR starchitect, and friend of Bertolt Brecht, Hermann Henselmann (1905–95), who also designed the Haus des Lehrers and neighbouring Congress Hall (now Berliner Congress Center) at Alexanderplatz.

Karl-Marx-Allee is 90 metres (295 feet) wide and 2.5 kilometres (1½ miles) long, and contemporary street life is swallowed somewhat by the grand scale of the planners' vision. That said, the avenue is still a favourite among tourists of Soviet monumentalism who flock to see what Italian architect and theorist Aldo Rossi (1931–97) proclaimed to be 'Europe's last great true street.'

The former Stalinallee has two distinct sections: the monumental 1950s Stalinist *Zuckerbäckerstil* architecture of the eastern end gives way to the International Style favoured in the 1960s in the later stretch closer to Alexanderplatz, where the street ends in the arresting ensemble of the Haus des Reisens, Haus des Lehrers, Kino International, Café Moskau and the BCC Kongresshalle designed by Hermann Henselmann et al.

# KINO INTERNATIONAL
A cinema for the cinephile

Designed by Josef Kaiser (1910–91) and Heinz Aust (b. 1927) as the main cinema for official East German movie premieres, the Kino International is one of the finest examples of International Style architecture in Europe. It opened in 1963 as East Berlin's answer to the giant Zoo Palast in the West. But unlike the Zoo Palast, whose interior was modernized almost beyond recognition, the Kino International retains a wealth of period details both inside and out. It is a real pleasure to experience the building as it was originally intended to be: original wood panelling, auditorium ceiling, door handles, chandeliers...right down to the hand-painted posters advertising the main feature film outside.

The Kino International is one of the last examples of a free-standing, single-screen cinema in the *Lichtspielhaus* or picture palace tradition – the precursor to the cinema-supermarket style of the multiplex we are familiar with today.

Berlin, by the way, has several amazing historic independent cinemas. Hans Poelzig's 1920s Babylon in Mitte, which is the last remaining large cinema in the city from the silent era – complete with orchestra pit – or the deep-red Delphi in Charlottenburg that was converted from an old dance hall in 1948 and looks like something out of a David Lynch film.

The foyer bar of the Kino International with a splendid view towards the Café Moskau opposite is a great place to drink a pre-film vodka and imagine yourself starring in a Cold War spy thriller.

# BERLIN'S STREET SIGN FONTS
## Signs of the times

Like Johnston in London or Helvetica in New York, every great city needs its iconic font. And of course Berlin has two of them.

The first, which came into use shortly after the Greater Berlin area was defined in 1920, was a variation on Jakob Erbar's seminal Erbar Grotesk font – one of the first geometric sans serif typefaces ever created. Combining easy legibility with subtle quirks such as the beautifully sharp *eszett* (ß) and a lovely combined 'tz' for common words like *Platz* (square), the new font gave 19th-century city streets a recognizably modern makeover.

After division came to the city, the GDR created a new urban visual identity and a new font for their renamed streets, which now honoured communist heroes such as Rosa Luxembourg and Ho Chi Minh. The *Ostfont* (East font) was distinguishable from its predecessor by its round edges and somewhat skinnier appearance. Some joked that the slimmed-down typeface was a result of the general scarcity of goods and materials in East Germany, but the more likely reason is that a narrower type was needed just to fit some of the epic street names such as Stadion der Weltjugend (Youth of the World Stadium) or Allee der Kosmonauten (Avenue of the Cosmonauts) onto the street signs.

In Berlin there are two of everything and typefaces are no exception. The street signs in the former East feature a narrow sans serif typeface known as *Ostfont* – designer unknown. In the former West, street signs still tend to feature Erbar Grotesk, with its beautiful fused 'tz' and equally distinctive 'ß', or 'sharp s'.

# FUNKHAUS NALEPASTRASSE AND HAUS DES RUNDFUNKS
Broadcasting in stereo

In the ideological conflicts that defined Germany through much of the 20th century, radio broadcasting was of crucial importance. Little surprise then that the broadcasting houses that fed entertainment, information and propaganda to the German people through the Weimar, Nazi, East and West German and post-reunification periods of the city's history have an architectural quality that befits their symbolic significance.

In the west end of the city sits the Haus des Rundfunks (Broadcasting House). Designed by Hans Poelzig (1869–1936), it was the first purpose-built broadcasting house in the world upon its completion in 1930 and would later serve as the most vital propaganda tool for the Nazi party with some of Goebbels' most famous speeches broadcast from its studios.

After the Second World War a new, second Funkhaus (Radio Building) was designed by communist architect Franz Ehrlich (1907–84) and built in 1950 all the way across town in the eastern sector of the city to broadcast stations such as Berliner Rundfunk and Radio DDR 1 to the East German people.

Despite their supposed rivalry, the two buildings are both closely related to Bauhaus architecture, with their rectilinear forms, ribbon windows and intricate masonry. Similarly, both are highly functional – the long straight façade of the west-end building serves to block traffic noise from the interior studios, while the eastern building contains the largest recording studio in Europe.

Berlin's two main broadcasting houses – Hans Poelzig's Haus des Rundfunks in the west (below) and Funkhaus Nalepastraße in the east (opposite) – are still flourishing. Thanks to their excellent acoustics, their concert halls are much treasured recording and performance venues for orchestras and bands alike.

# THE PREGNANT OYSTER
What's in a name?

Berlin's tourist guides have an annoying tendency to supply you with the nicknames Berliners supposedly ascribe to their iconic landmarks. The Haus der Kulturen der Welt (House of the World's Cultures), situated in the Tiergarten on the banks of the River Spree, has several to choose from and inspired other names in turn. Built in 1957, it quickly acquired the nickname *Die schwangere Auster* (The Pregnant Oyster), thanks to the signature sweeping, International Style architecture of its roof.

It was designed as a congress hall by the American architect Hugh Stubbins (1912–2006) as a gift to Germany from the United States for the 1957 International Building Exhibition in the nearby Hansaviertel. The open arch of the shell-shaped, concrete roof, which has some resemblance to a broad grin, later inspired a second nickname, *Jimmy Carter's Lächeln* (Jimmy Carter's Smile). And in the 1980s, when part of the roof collapsed, it inspired the name of one of West Berlin's most famous bands, the industrial music legends Einstürzende Neubauten (Collapsing New Buildings).

Today it is just called the HKW (pronounced 'ha-ka-vay') and is Germany's national centre for the presentation and discussion of contemporary arts, with one of the most exciting and innovative arts programmes in Europe.

Besides being an important landmark right next to Berlin's government district, the HKW is one of Germany's leading contemporary arts institutions whose programme, festivals and events are an important feature for the contemporary art scene, not just in Berlin.

# BAHNHOF ZOO
## West Berlin's dark anti-icon

A clumsy and ugly building, the Berlin Zoologischer Garten train station is certainly no design icon, in fact it's quite the opposite. Its history has been a succession of fails right from the start. In 1934, Hitler's Germany decided to remove the 19th-century original and replace it with a modern one for the 1936 Olympic Games. A familiar tale from other large public-transport projects in Berlin, corners were cut in the rush to try and get it finished on time and, as a result, the building was cheaply and poorly constructed. Worse still: only five years after its inauguration in a half-completed state, it was severely damaged by Allied bombing.

In 1957 the reconstruction and expansion of Bahnhof Zoo, as it is known locally, failed to make the building any prettier. Out of necessity, and because of the lack of any other large train station in its city centre, it became West Berlin's central rail hub for all connections to Western Germany, although it was never intended for such a task.

In the 1970s and 1980s, the station became the central meeting point for West Berlin's drug scene and this unfortunate and awkward building gained even greater notoriety as the backdrop for the bestselling book, then film, *Christiane F – We Children From Bahnhof Zoo*, the grim, disturbing biography of an under-aged girl who becomes addicted to heroin and then ends up as prostitute plying her trade in the harshly lit belly of the station. The building has since lost its importance as a hub to the new Hauptbahnhof central station further up the line and, despite various attempted facelifts and clean-ups, it remains one of those icons of historical awkwardness that make Berlin what it is.

The soundtrack to the 1981 film *Christiane F – Wir Kinder vom Bahnhof Zoo* consists entirely of songs written by David Bowie when he lived in the nearby district of Schöneberg between 1976 and 1979. He composed his so-called Berlin Trilogy of albums here during that time: *Low* (1977), *Heroes* (1977) and *Lodger* (1979).

# THE LITTLE GREEN MEN
Little men, big comeback

Berlin's streets have seen their fair share of battles in their time but few outside Germany might be aware of one that involved a horde of little red and green men. We are not talking about extra-terrestrial visitors here, but an East/West dispute over the pictogram walk/don't walk light signals at pedestrian crossings, known affectionately as *Ampelmännchen* (little traffic light men) in former East Germany.

The 1961 design of the GDR *Ampelmännchen* was proposed by Karl Peglau (1927–2009), a practitioner in the field of traffic psychology, who suggested that pedestrians respond best to clearly defined, 'positive' crossing symbols. Hence, the cheerful, striding man wearing a hat (supposedly inspired by a clip on East German TV of Erich Honecker, the then secretary for security of the ruling Socialist Unity Party, wearing a straw hat). This was in contrast to the more understated, generic figures seen on crossings in West Berlin at the time. After reunification an attempt was made to standardize to the Western model in the 1990s – but certain citizens revolted.

The psychological associations of the *Ampelmännchen* extend far beyond traffic; they are synonymous with *Ostalgie*, nostalgia for the defunct East German state. As the *Ampelmännchen* started being replaced, their cause was picked up by an industrial designer from southern Germany named Markus Heckhausen, who began buying up old examples and creating merchandise in the form of lamps to highlight their disappearance. A campaign to reinstate them gained momentum and the authorities relented, allowing one key piece of East German identity at least to live on.

Walk, don't walk: the strict attention Berliners tend to pay to their pedestrian traffic signals can be a source of amusement for some visitors. Citizens can often be seen patiently waiting for the signal to turn green before crossing – even when there is not a single car in sight.

# TEUFELSBERG
The hills have ears

Teufelsberg (Devil's Mountain) is a 120-metre- (394-foot-) high artificial hill in the Grünewald forest made from some of the 75 million square metres (81 million square feet) of building rubble cleared mainly by hand by legions of *Trümmerfrauen* (literally, 'rubble women') from the bomb-ravaged city after the war.

During the Cold War it became the site of a field station to listen to Soviet chatter emanating from East Berlin and beyond. Established by the US National Security Agency (NSA) in 1961 just months before the Wall went up, by 1963 the facility had been made permanent, with a distinctive structure comprising three globes, each of which housed an antenna.

Now derelict, dilapidated and surrounded by forest, 'The Hill', as it was known by those who worked there, is currently in the midst of a stalemate rather befitting its Cold War origins; the city is too poor to buy the thing back and do something with it, while the developers who own it can't build anything because the site now falls under forest preservation orders. There is no shortage of suggestions as to what to do with one of the city's most distinctive landmarks: at one point the film director David Lynch had plans to turn the site into a centre for transcendental meditation.

Derelict but not unused: the Teufelsberg is a great place to watch the sunset and the site has become a favourite of urban explorers. Its slopes are used by mountain bikers and it serves as a good tobogganing run in the winter.

# RINGBAHN
Circling the city by train

A favourite activity of tired wanderers in need of a nap or Berliners in search of some contemplation time is to 'ride the ring': a 37-kilometre (23-mile) S-Bahn loop that encircles the city centre and forms an informal boundary between the inner city neighbourhoods and those regions 'outside the ring'.

With the first sections constructed between Moabit and Gesundbrunnen in 1871, the circle was completed with the laying of tracks through the then independent city of Charlottenburg by 1877. The loop was, however, broken again with the physical division of the city by the East German government in 1961. Although the eastern section of the railway line continued to run between Schönhauser Allee and Treptower Park throughout the Cold War, the western section was the subject of a politically motivated boycott as all the revenue from the line went to the East German government. When restoration of the ring was completed in June 2002, it was a symbolic moment for the reunification process of the once divided city.

Today, despite the occasional grumble from morning commuters, the Ringbahn runs more or less smoothly, with each train circumnavigating the city in 60 minutes. At the weekend when Berlin's public transport runs all night, the Ringbahn acts as a giant clock, spinning continuously, both clockwise and counterclockwise, counting away the hours in a city that rarely sleeps.

Owing to its irregular shape, the central Berlin city Ringbahn public transport loop is also known locally as the *Hundekopf* (dog's head). The occupation of Germany by the allied forces ended in 1949, but on the 1959 East German S-Bahn map (opposite), the French, British and American sectors of Berlin are still indicated by the letters F, B and A; the Soviet sector is marked D for Deutschland, as the GDR still considered West Berlin an occupied zone at the time.

Schulzendorf (b Tegel)
Bln=Hermsdorf
104
104d
Blankenfelde
106
Bln=Karow
105
Bln=Tegel
Waidmannslust
Wittenau (Nordb)
Bln=Rosenthal
Bln=
Wilhelmsruh
100b
Bln=
Blankenburg
103c
Eichbornstr
Bln=Reinickendorf
Wittenau
(Kremm Bahn)
105
Bln=
Schönholz
104
105
106
Pankow=Heinersdorf
104c
F
Wollankstr
Bln=Pankow
Gesundbrunnen
Bornholmer Str
100b
Schönhauser Allee
D
tenfeld
100a
Bln=Wedding
100/103a
Prenzlauer Allee
st
100c
Bln=Siemensstadt
PuHitzstr
Humboldthain
Greifswalder Str
Spandau
Wernerwerk 100
103a
BeuBelstr
104
Nordbahnhof
100a
Leninallee
iemensstadt-
urstenbrunn
Jungfernheide
Lehrter Stadtbf
105
Oranienburger Str
100
Zentralviehhof
100
Bellevue
103
106
100b
103a
103
B
Westend
Triergarten
102
Unter
den Linden
Marx=Engels=Platz
101 102
Alexanderplatz
Stalinallee
101d
100a
101a, 101
Bln
Savigny-
Potsdamer
Pl
Bln
Friedrichstr
103
Jannowitzbr
100a Warschauer
106b 104c
Fri
100
Witzleben
platz
Zoolog.Garten
104
Bln Ostbahnhof
101a
Str 100b
102c
Bln=Licht
eerstr
Bln=
Charlottenbg.
105
106
Anhalter Bf
Ostkreuz
Nöldnerplatz
101
chkamp
Westkreuz
100/103/103a
102c
Rummelsburg
101/102
Bln=Halensee
Großgörschen
Str
Yorckstr
Treptower Park
106b
Betriebsbf
newald
100
Hohenzollern
damm
104
105
106
103
102d
102
Karlsho
Schmargendf
Schöneberg
100
106c
Plänterwald
101a
Bln=Wilmersdorf
Innsbrucker Platz
Papestr
Sonnenallee
103a
Baumschulenw
Schlachtensee
Feuerbachstr
Bln=Steglitz
Fried-
denau
Bln=
Tempelhof
Bln=Neukölln
Hermannstr
101a
101a
103
Oberspree
104
Bln=Lichterf West
104
Botan
Garten
Priesterweg
100/101a
Köllnischeheide
Bln=Schöneweide
103a
thaler
Allee
A
106
105
Mariendorf
102c
Betriebsbf B
Bln=Adler
Bln=Sundgauer Str
Südende
106b
104a
Zehlendorf
Lank-
witz
Bln=Marienfelde
105a
101a/1
Bln=
chnow
Lichterfelde Ost
Buckower
Chaussee
10
Lichterfelde Süd
106
106a
Teltow
Lichtenrade
orf
Großbeeren
106c
106c
Mahlow
102c 106b
Abnordendorf
Blankenfelde (b. Zossen)

# THE BERLIN PHILHARMONIC
## Hans Scharoun's 'nautical' concert hall

The Berliner Philharmonie (Berlin Philharmonic), built between 1960 and 1963, is considered a masterpiece of expressionist modernism. Designed by Hans Scharoun (1893–1972), it is part of the Kulturforum, a complex of buildings that also includes his Staatsbibliothek (State Library) and Mies van der Rohe's Neue Nationalgalerie (see page 56). Scharoun, a contemporary of the Bauhaus generation but with greatly differing views on architecture, believed passionately in what he called 'organic building': a democratic architecture for the community, developing the concept of a city landscape, which should grow from the bottom up, arising from the needs of the community.

Scharoun's design for the Berlin Philharmonic was based upon a simple but revolutionary premise: that the music should be at the centre. The 2,442 seats of the main hall are arranged in a pattern of raked terraces around the podium in what has become known as a 'vineyard' formation. The combination of these terraces and the prominent diffusion reflector surfaces in wood, stone and fibreglass aid the acoustics. The foyer wraps around the hall and is a maze of multilevel decks, bridges, steps and parapets with round porthole-shapes in the architect's trademark nautical style. It is not what one would call a beautiful building – the apparent jumble of planes and angles are hard work on the eye – but sit inside during a concert and the architecture springs into vibrant life as it fulfils its purpose: the unification of space, music and people.

Music in the round: Hans Scharoun's democratic and humanist design was intended to avoid hierarchies and allow the members of the audience to feel like they are sharing the room with each other and the orchestra. Herbert von Karajan, head of the Berlin Philharmonic in the 1960s and instrumental in choosing Scharoun's design for the new concert hall, apparently threatened to leave Berlin if this building was not chosen.

# NEUE NATIONALGALERIE
Mies' minimalist masterstroke

Many great minds fled Germany during the years of the Nazi regime, and one of the pioneers of modern architecture was among them. Ludwig Mies van der Rohe (1886–1969) who had served as the last director of the Bauhaus, left Germany in 1937 to find a new home in the United States. This loss for German architecture was made all the more clear with his spectacular return to Berlin for one last creative masterstroke in 1965.

With the New National Gallery, completed a year before he died (he never actually saw the completed building), Mies gave the city one of his most spectacular buildings. Its floating, black rectilinear presence is an extraordinary combination of lightness and weight, of impact and invisibility. Its effect is further enhanced by its proximity to the dancing, golden-roofed ensemble of Hans Scharoun's Philharmonie and Staatsbibliothek next door (see page 54).

Mies' minimalist modernist building is dominated by a roof that seems to hover above the upper main hall. It is supported by just eight slender pillars on the outside, away from the corners, which allows for a spectacular, high-ceilinged, universal presentation space which is used for special exhibitions and concerts. The rest of the building, reserved for the permanent collection of modern art up until the 1970s, lies below ground and is open to daylight via a sunken sculpture garden behind the building.

The Neue Nationalgalerie is closed until around 2020 for a complete renovation but it is still worth a visit to enjoy the expressive sculptural quality of the building alone. While the gallery is closed, its collection can be viewed at the Hamburger Bahnhof, a contemporary art gallery near Berlin's main train station.

# AXEL SPRINGER BUILDING
Trophy architecture at its finest

Rumour has it that Axel Springer (1912–85), founder and owner of the largest publishing empire in postwar Germany, personally drew a sketch of this building while approaching West Berlin by plane in 1961. From above, he saw the Berlin Wall for the first time and decided that his new high-rise headquarters, under construction right next to the Wall needed to be a gleaming, gloating symbol of the freedom and wealth of the West, a 'cry against the wind' that would shine its light far into the dark, communist East.

The building complex actually consists of three sections, but this elegantly modern high-rise clearly is the most prominent. At 68 metres (223 feet) in height, its eye-catching façade of gold-coloured aluminium sheets covers two sides of the building. When it opened in 1966, there was no doubt about what this golden edifice was meant to express.

After 1990, the shine had become a little tarnished, the tower was renovated and a massive new wing was added, a very transparent building with apparently no further symbolism intended. At the time of writing, another large expansion is under construction situated right on the former 'death strip' of the Wall and designed by Rem Koolhaas' (b. 1944) OMA studio.

On the 19th floor of this golden high-rise, there is an exclusive journalists' club reserved for VIPs. The walls of this room are lined with another of Axel Springer's trophies: original wood panelling from the offices of *The Times* in London. Mikhail Gorbachev, the Dalai Lama, George Bush, Helmut Kohl and Billy Wilder have all been guests here.

# UMLAUFTANK 2
A techno-magical legacy

This is one of the strangest buildings in Berlin. Designed by architect Ludwig Leo (1924–2012) and completed in 1975, the Umlauftank 2 (Circulation Tank 2) is a research complex for water and shipbuilding belonging to the Technical University of Berlin. Poking out above the trees of the Tiergarten, it is a blue laboratory building with a green chimney being pushed skywards by giant pink water pipes. It looks like a peculiar robotic animal that you would almost expect to move up and down, maybe gently breathing with the fluctuation of the water inside.

Mysteries aside, this is a purely technical construction: a huge tunnel for researching ship hydrodynamics and conducting navigational engineering tests with scaled model ships. Two diesel engines pump water through the colossal 8-metre- (26-foot)-diameter pink pipes. The building contains a number of water basins that simulate different wave conditions and currents. Leo did not build many buildings, but with all of them he made the technical requirements the main feature of his architecture, in this case, by not hiding the pipes but placing them outside and painting them pink. It's Berlin's Centre Pompidou in this respect. By transforming the technical into a much greater gesture, Leo has left a techno-magical legacy to the city.

The colour scheme of the Umlauftank 2 (shown here in 1977) matches that of the numerous giant pink pipes dotted around the city. Berlin has a very high water table and when foundations are dug for new buildings, in order to prevent the site from flooding the water has to be continuously pumped away – in pink pipes, of course.

# TV TOWER
Tower of signals and signifiers

Berlin's distinctive TV Tower is everywhere. Not just because it looms above the majority of the city's buildings that still adhere to a 19th-century height restriction or because it somehow manages to peek out behind and upstage those buildings that don't, but also because its distinctive silhouette adorns much of Berlin's branding paraphernalia and tourist souvenirs.

Completed in 1969, the Fernsehturm is the product of so many historical facets synonymous with the city – Cold War, Space Race, politics and design – all wrapped up in one architectural edifice. A 368-metre (1,207-foot) column topped by a sphere echoing the first Soviet space probe, *Sputnik*, and housing a revolving restaurant, it was the tallest structure in any part of Germany at the time: one big finger raised towards to the West by the East German regime.

But what East Berlin's chief architect Hermann Henselmann (1905–95), who named his concept design 'Tower of Signals' – no doubt fully aware that this tower would communicate more than just TV and radio broadcasts – most likely did not foresee is that his design would endure as the undisputed signifier, not just of unified Berlin, but perhaps Germany as a whole.

Much has changed in the city since the 1960s, but the TV Tower remains, a point of orientation for its inhabitants in the best tradition of the dogged tenacity of this city that has seen and withstood so much.

# DÖNER KEBAB
Berlin's culinary gift to the world

Surviving the city that never sleeps usually involves some fast-food intake during the small hours of the night – or at lunchtime on the go between appointments. Despite a steady increase in alternatives, for most citizens this usually means one of two things: *Currywurst* – chunks of sausage '*mit oder ohne darm*' (with or without skin) slathered in curry-flavoured ketchup – or a *Döner* kebab.

Berlin's growing Turkish community of 'guest workers' brought the kebab to Berlin back in the 1960s and 1970s, when (as the story goes) a man named Kadir Nurman customized the dish into the ubiquitous hand-sized pitta bread street food sandwich we know today. The now classic filling is a combination of spit-roasted minced meat, shredded lettuce, cabbage, tomato, '*mit oder ohne*' (with or without) onions and a choice of sauces – '*Scharf, Knoblauch oder Kräuter*' (spicy, garlic or herbs) – in 1972 at his fast-food stand near Zoo Station.

There are now over 1,000 *Döner* sellers in the city, which makes Berlin the *Döner* capital of Germany and *Döner*, by common consent, the number 1 fast food in the city. Is it Turkish or is it German? It's a wonderful mixture of both; a happily integrated and much-loved fusion from a community that has greatly enriched the fabric and sense of community in a city that can occasionally have grumpy tendencies – when hungry, at least.

Fast food with inbuilt salad. A night out in Berlin is incomplete without refuelling on a *Döner* at some point in the early hours.

# TOMMY-WEISBECKER-HAUS
## Punk rock doesn't do icons

This house is a survivor. First it survived the Second World War, then the subsequent demolition of most of the remaining buildings in this inner city area of Kreuzberg. In the following years it was just one of many empty buildings in West Berlin until, in 1973, a group of homeless youths squatted at a nearby alternative youth centre on Potsdamer Straße, the 'Drugstore', demanding a place to live. After protracted negotiations with the Senat (city government), they were offered this inconspicuous house on one of West Berlin's many dead-end streets cut off by the Wall. They moved in and named their new home after Thomas Weisbecker, a 23-year-old suspected of being involved with the violent anarchist group '2nd June Movement', who had just been shot dead by the German police in Augsburg. It is most likely the only house in Berlin named after an officially classified 'terrorist'.

Today the Tommyhaus, as it is known, is still a social centre offering accommodation for homeless youths, but it also has a bar, serves community meals and has a very nice little concert hall, known for its range of punk rock, ska and metal music. In the absence of any neighbouring buildings, the inhabitants painted spectacular murals on all four sides of the building in 1989, funded in part by the IBA International Building Exhibition. West Berlin in the 1980s was famous for its large numbers of punks and squatters. Today, as real-estate prices soar, the Tommyhaus is one of the last remaining landmarks of punk and disobedience in the city, and compared with other famous former squats like SO36 or Köpi, it is definitely the most beautiful.

Berlin's multinational street art culture is as legendary as it is superb. In addition to a long tradition of wall murals, the city's walls are also adorned with a wide variety of graffiti. Street art to look out for includes works by El Bocho, 1UP, X0000X, John Reaktor, Emess and Blu.

# BERLIN CLOCK
Ahead of its time

The 24-hour Weltzeituhr (World Time Clock) at Alexanderplatz might get all the tourist glory but my personal favourite civic timepiece in the city is the Berlin-Uhr (Berlin Clock), aka the Mengenlehreuhr (Set Theory Clock), which now stands in the Europa Centre on Budapester Straße. It was created by watchmaker and electrical engineer Dieter Binninger (1938–91) in 1975 for the city's 750th anniversary celebrations and, according to the *Guinness Book of Records*, was the first public clock in the world to tell the time using set theory. From 1975 to 1995 it stood on the Kurfürstendamm.

So how does one tell the time on a timepiece that doubles as a lightshow? Start at the top and read row by row. Each light in the top red row represents 5 hours, each light in the bottom red row represents 1 hour. Add those together and you get the time in 24-hour format. Still following? For minutes, the same principle applies: each light in the upper yellow row represents 5 minutes (indicated in red are 15, 30 and 45 minutes) and on the lower row, each light represents 1 minute. The blinking circular light counts the seconds. Add that all together and it's probably quite some time since you started but, hey, isn't maths fun?

Telling the time on the Mengenlehreuhr: the red lights of the top row denote 5 hours each and those of the second row a full hour, while the lights on the third row indicate 5 minutes each and those on the bottom row 1 minute. So the time shown in this photograph is 18:08 (or 8 minutes past 6pm).

# BIERPINSEL
Berlin 'brut' in Steglitz

Towering 47 metres (154 feet) above Schloßstraße U-Bahn station in the south-western district of Steglitz, this Pop Art-meets-Brutalism oddity is just the kind of unholy architectural mash-up that seems right at home in this city. Officially inaugurated as Turmrestaurant Steglitz (Tower Restaurant Steglitz), it's universally known to Berliners as the Bierpinsel (beer brush), a moniker that supposedly originates from the free beer the once-bright red 'tavern in a tower' served at its opening on 13 October 1976.

Construction took four years and was the first built project by the husband and wife team of Ralf Schüler (1930–2011) and Ursulina Schüler-Witte (b. 1933), better know for their later West Berlin centrepiece, the Internationales Congress Centrum Berlin (ICC), one of the biggest congress centres in the world when it was finished in 1979 but which was closed in 2014.

Having been variously used as a restaurant, nightclub and art space, the Bierpinsel's doors have also been officially shut since 2006 but its fate is not yet sealed. At the time of writing it is clad in a multicoloured collage of street art, thanks to Turmkunst 2010, an initiative that handed over the structure as a canvas to four internationally renowned graffiti artists – Flying Förtress, Honet, Sozyone and Craig 'KR' Costello – to decorate as they wished.

The 1970s Turmrestaurant Steglitz, known to all as the Bierpinsel, once contained three floors of restaurants and a nightclub. Currently closed, it remains to be seen whether the building will be restored to its former spacey glory or fall victim to Berlin's patchy gentrification programme.

# SCHAUBÜHNE THEATRE
Expressionist theatre

Today it is one of Berlin's most radical and experimental theatres, but the Schaubühne am Lehniner Platz (Playhouse on Lehniner Square) was actually built as a cinema. It was designed as part of a much larger entity called the WOGA complex, which contained apartment buildings, a restaurant, tennis courts and a little shopping street, parts of which you can still see behind the building today. The highlight of the complex was the cinema Universum situated at the upper end of Kurfürstendamm. It opened in 1928 with a 1,800-seat capacity, which was enormous for a cinema at that time.

Designed by the Expressionist architect Erich Mendelsohn (1887–1953) – most famous for his organically shaped Einsteinturm (1922) in Potsdam – the building consists of two curved brick volumes stacked upon each other to create a stunning contrast between the heaviness of the material and the dynamics of the form. Jutting out above is a massive ventilation shaft that appears to slice the building in half.

The building was heavily damaged in the Second World War and it took until 1981 to restore it completely. Berlin architect Jürgen Sawade (1927–2015) accurately reconstructed the historic exterior while transforming the interior into one of Germany's most technically advanced theatres. Known now as the Schaubühne, it has hosted directors such as Peter Stein (b. 1937), Luc Bondy (1948–2015), Robert Wilson (b. 1941) and Sasha Waltz (b. 1963) in the successful continuation of its radically innovative tradition.

Brecht and beyond: Berlin's theatre landscape, particularly the experimental, avant-garde and independent, is one of the richest in Europe. And it has some great theatres to match. As well as the Schaubühne, shown here newly restored in 1982, the Schiller Theater, Volksbühne, Maxim Gorki Theater and the Deutsche Oper are all also worth a visit for their buildings alone.

# KREUZBERG TOWER
At home with Hejduk

The American architect-cum-theorist-cum-poet John Hejduk (1929–2000) is remembered more for his contributions to architectural drawing, research and education (his former pupils include Daniel Libeskind and Liz Diller) than for his built forms, which makes his Kreuzberg Tower on Charlottenstraße all the more special.

Built in 1987 as part of the Internationale Bauausstellung (International Architecture Exhibition), this mixed-use structure stands out in glorious isolation amid an otherwise densely built-up neighbourhood. The 14-storey tower (originally designed to contain artists' studios) and its stouter sidewings (containing 55 social housing units) are characterized by their unusual façade features. Its green metallic balconies and sunshades give the ensemble an anthropomorphic quality.

Inside the tower, apartments are divided between cavernous central rooms at the core of the building and boxy extensions at its edges, prompting those who live there to muse on Hejduk's intriguing (if slightly impractical) interplay of architectural forms.

The ensemble has been threatened with 'modernization' in recent years, only to be repeatedly saved by outpourings of affection from the international architecture community: the Japanese architect Shigeru Ban (b. 1957) described the Kreuzberg Tower as 'a message of selflessness in a world so often dominated by greed.'

The 1987 IBA architecture exhibition held in West Berlin was a postmodernist showcase prioritizing social housing and planning. It also included one of the late Zaha Hadid's first ever buildings, IBA Block B on Stresemannstraße, an angular precursor to her later works.

# BERLIN WALL MEMORIAL
Remembering the divided city

Separating the two halves of the city, the Berlin Wall reflected in one city what the Cold War did, not just to Germany, but to the whole of Europe. From the moment the first concrete slabs went up in 1961, until the night of 9 November 1989, it was an ever-expanding monstrosity. In 28 years the Wall grew into a 162-kilometre- (100-mile-) long ring with a floodlit, razor-wired 'death strip' in front up to 500 metres (1,600 feet) wide.

It was supposed to keep the 'fascists' out, but everybody knew the Berlin Wall was built to keep the GDR's own citizens in. Border guards were ordered to 'shoot to kill' defectors and well over a hundred people lost their lives in the attempt.

Beyond the colourfully painted section known as the East Side Gallery, today there is little left to see where the Wall once stood and, visually at least, many of the divided city's scars have healed. To really understand the sense of threat Berliners lived under at the time, visit the Berlin Wall Memorial on Bernauer Straße, a remarkable 1.4-kilometre- (³/4-mile-) long open-air museum and 'memorial landscape' between Brunnenstraße and Gartenstraße. Structures of particular note here are the Chapel of Reconciliation, built from stamped earth made from the rubble of a demolished church on the site, and an original section of the Wall – complete with 'death strip', razor wire and watch tower.

# STOLPERSTEINE
Stumbling over Berlin's dark past

In Berlin, there are two very different styles of memorial to the crimes of Nazi Germany that play important roles in Germany's obligation to remember. There are the formal memorials, such as the Memorial to the Murdered Jews of Europe near the Brandenburg Gate, or the nearby memorials to the Sinti and Roma and to homosexuals persecuted under the Nazis. And then there is the *Stolpersteine* (stumbling stones) project, a privately initiated memorial commemorating individual lives lost. Started in 1992 by Berlin-born artist Gunter Demnig (b. 1947), the project has since expanded to several European cities, incorporating over 32,000 individual stones to date.

Whereas one could intentionally bypass the big central memorials to the horror that was planned and executed in this city, as a tourist and as a Berliner one cannot ignore these small but effective everyday reminders of individual stories that too often get lost in the bigger perspective. Scattered all over the city, in front of ordinary houses, small engraved brass cobblestones are set into the ground, each bearing a brief inscription. Each begins with the words '*Hier wohnte...*' ('Here lived…'), followed by the name, birth date and the fate of the individual: '...deported Auschwitz, 1943, murdered' or '...humiliated, vilified, dead 8.1.1943'. The *Stolpersteine* are deeply moving in their shocking brevity – whole lives marked by only a handful of words.

Berlin's 'stumbling stones': poignant reminders of millions of individual tragedies that happened to so many families in so many streets all over Europe between 1933 and 1945.

HIER WOHNTE
ANITA BUKOFZER
JG. 1930
DEPORTIERT 1943
ERMORDET IN
AUSCHWITZ

HIER WOHNTE
URY
DAVIDSOHN
JG. 1943
DEPORTIERT 1943
THERESIENSTADT
ERMORDET IN
AUSCHWITZ

HIER WOHNTE
PAULA
DAVIDSOHN
GEB. KATZ
JG. 1905
DEPORTIERT 1943
THERESIENSTADT
ERMORDET IN
AUSCHWITZ

# VOLKSBÜHNE VISUAL IDENTITY
Playing against type

Spend just a short while perusing the fly-postered and graffitied walls that act as a backdrop to the streets of Berlin and a distinctive series of bold posters will begin to demand your attention – featuring words and phrases such as 'GAME OVER', 'LÜGE' (lie) and 'KRISE' (crisis) in a Gothic script typeface, sometimes against a hyperactive fluorescent background, sometimes just plain black and white.

Provocative theatre requires provocative graphics. The Volksbühne opened its doors in 1914 with a mission to deliver 'naturalist plays at prices accessible to the common worker'. Its legendary director Frank Castorf ran the house from 1992 until the end of 2016.

These strange missives advertise the activities of the legendary Volksbühne (People's Theatre), which was founded in the 1920s to make the politically imbued theatre of the day accessible to Berlin's working classes. Still housed in its original building in Mitte, designed by Oskar Kaufmann (1873–1956), the institution still enjoys, and often plays up to, its reputation as the *enfant terrible* of the city's five state-funded theatres.

The provocative choice to employ a branding strategy with powerfully Teutonic visuals (the blackletter typeface Fraktur was a favourite of Hitler's) was the brainchild of the Volksbühne's chief set designer, the late Bert Neumann (1960–2015), whose Berlin-based design studio LSD created the campaign in 2013. Neumann was also responsible for the theatre's distinctive Räuber-Rad (robber wheel) logo, which was designed in 1992 following a radical new production of Friedrich Schiller's famous 1782 work *Die Räuber* (*The Robbers*).

Repurposed, rougher around the edges and operating in a vastly different contemporary context, this is a visual identity that neatly encapsulates the synchronicity between an institution renowned for going off script and its adopted typeface.

# TECHNO
The beat goes on

Techno may have been born in Detroit but it certainly grew up in Berlin. What began with the opening up of abandoned spaces in East Berlin for parties, following the fall of the Wall, grew into a citywide, or rather global, phenomenon by the late 1990s when over a million people would take over the Tiergarten streets annually for DJs Dr Motte and Westbam's infamous Love Parade.

The transient nature of the city provided the perfect environment for the growth of a scene that thrived on spontaneity, movement, 120–150bpm and, let's face it, a great deal of chemical stimulants. Iconic clubs such as E-Werk and Tresor came and went, only to be replaced by today's Berghain or //:about blank, which continue to provide the next generation of revellers with nightlife culture that is as much about social and sexual freedom as it is about hedonism.

While the increasing influx of nightlife tourists – the much bemoaned 'Easyjetset' which began arriving in the mid-Noughties – has been blamed for the commercialization of the scene, there is little sign that the city is losing its touch for progressive sounds. Born out of techno, postdigital music represents the new electronic avant-garde and with it comes new spaces that are open to more fluid gender and sexual identities than earlier scenes. As ever, the beat goes on.

DJ Haito doing his thing in Club Maria in Friedrichshain (top). This mainly techno club closed in 2011 but not before being immortalized in the (highly recommended) feature film *Berlin Calling*. Ritter Butzke in Kreuzberg (bottom) started off as an illegal venue in 2007 but is now official and a local favourite.

# TEGEL AIRPORT
## The six-sided wonder of Berlin

In the era of endless waiting for the scandal-ridden, blunder-afflicted national embarrassment that is the new Berlin Brandenburg International airport (BER), originally due for completion in 2010, Berliners have perhaps never loved their old Tegel Airport more. This is because they can continue to enjoy the hexagonal delights of what is one of the most efficient airport designs in the world. Tegel's main terminal building is arranged around an open square into which passengers arrive before passing through gate-specific check-ins, passport control and security services ahead of boarding their plane just metres away.

If or when BER opens for business, Tegel Airport is due to close, with one proposal looking to turn this architecturally innovative transport hub into a start-up tech innovation hub instead.

This typically German exercise in efficiency was designed by Meinhard von Gerkan (b. 1935) and Volkwin Marg (b. 1936) in 1965 and completed in 1975 – it was their very first commission. The site's connection with the air dates back to the early 20th century when it was a location for Prussian airship tests. Later, at the height of the Soviet blockade of Berlin in 1948, a runway was built in just 90 days. Tegel began welcoming commercial traffic in the 1950s, but only airlines from the occupying powers because of the special status of West Berlin airspace.

Officially named Flughafen Berlin-Tegel 'Otto Lilienthal' (TXL) in 1988, after the 19th-century German aviation pioneer, by 2015 the airport comprised five terminals serving some 21 million passengers annually, but it is due to close as soon as BER is open for business. Here's hoping for a stay of execution for this wonderfully fast and queue-free city hub.

# HACKESCHE HÖFE
Courtyard life behind the streets

'These courtyards exhale the essence of the city'. Wim Wenders

Today this series of eight interconnecting courtyards, between Rosenthaler Straße and Sophienstraße, originally designed by Kurt Berndt (1863–1925) in 1906, is on the main tourist drag of Berlin Mitte, adjacent to the Hackescher Markt: its attractions ranging from the very fine Art Nouveau architecture of the tiled first courtyard, designed by August Engell (1871–1925), to the silversmiths and shoe makers in courtyard number VII.

The bustle here reflects the nature of Berlin's commercial heart, which has once again regained the energy it had when the courtyards were built and Berlin was one of the most densely populated cities in Europe, particularly in this district known as the Spandauer Vorstadt.

The 27,000 square-metre (29,000 square-feet) block, one of the largest and finest examples of the courtyard building system in Germany, was originally designed to incorporate 80 apartments as well as offices, small factories and, in the front two courtyards, entertainment facilities including a theatre and public ballrooms. It was designed so as to allow light and air into the living spaces and courtyards, some of which had seating areas and fountains, and to help improve the health of the city's residents, living in overcrowded conditions where tuberculosis was rife.

Following a complete renovation in the mid-1990s, this mixed-use format has remained and once again the Hackesche Höfe accommodate apartments, businesses, shops and public venues including a variety theatre, a cinema and a nightclub.

The Hackesche Höfe are a particularly attractive representative of the typical courtyard layout that cuts through so many blocks in Berlin – a city that only reveals itself fully once you step off the street to explore.

# JEWISH MUSEUM
Zigzagging through Jewish history

Love it or hate it, the Jewish Museum stands out as a remarkable building and is one of the very few really radical structures built in Berlin after reunification. While the rest of the post-Wall city succumbed to the stone-clad banality of retro-historic façades, this zigzagging silver thunderbolt was making its mark in Kreuzberg – and the reputation of its architect with it. Daniel Libeskind (b. 1946) actually won the competition for the new museum just before the fall of the Wall in 1989 but, because of the resulting political and financial upheavals, the Jewish Museum did not open until 2001.

A first surprise for the visitor is that you cannot actually enter this building from the street, but have to go in via an underground passage leading from the baroque building next door – which actually is Berlin's Jewish Museum, and has been since 1971. Libeskind's building, though considerably larger, is only an 'extension'. Beginning with this remarkable connection between the old and the new, Libeskind's design is bursting with strong symbolic meaning: underground access, weirdly slanted walls and empty voids among the exhibition spaces all reflect the intensity of the inescapable historical context. The building is more than a museum, it is a monument in itself. Maybe that is why the architecture was at its most convincing when the building was first opened to the public in 1999 – completely empty.

Daniel Libeskind's deconstructivist architecture is so dominant that one of the largest Jewish museums in Europe has ended up more of a sculpture than a receptacle for the permanent exhibition of 'two millennia of German Jewish history'.

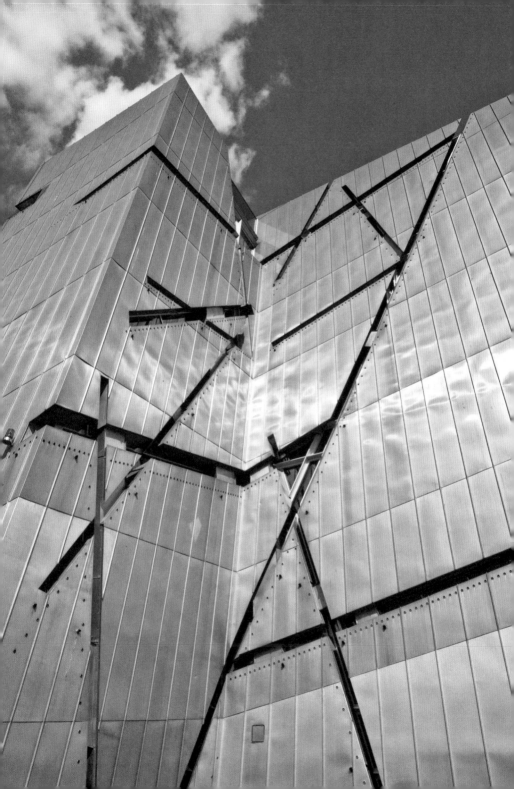

# TEMPODROM

From anarchic roots to luxurious leisure pursuits

The Tempodrom began as a circus tent pitched on the razed Potsdamer Platz on 1 May 1980 when Irene Moessinger, a local nurse with a squatter background who had received a sizeable inheritance, decided to use her money to found a venue to host events from the alternative music and theatre scene, which was in rude health at the time. Four years later her circus tent upped pegs and moved to the Tiergarten, next to the HKW (see page 44) and not far from what was once a historic street named In den Zelten (in the tents), where 18th-century marquees had stood. Later it shifted again to make way for the new Federal Chancellery and, as of 2002, now exists in 'permanent' form on the site of what was once the main hall of the vast Anhalter Bahnhof, a fragment of which is still standing nearby.

Reminiscent of an Oscar Niemeyer (1907–2012) building from Brasilia, the expressive form of the building's roof – a competition-winning design by Meinhard von Gerkan (b. 1935), whose architecture firm Von Gerkan, Marg und Partner (gmp) was already known for its revolutionary hexagonal Tegel Airport (see page 84) – neatly references its circular circus origins. More recently, gmp designed Berlin's new Hauptbahnhof (main train station).

Today the Tempodrom hosts a broader, rather more commercial and less anarchic programme than it did in its early days. The building's basement now houses a luxury spa, the Liquidrom, complete with underwater light and 'soundscape'.

# BOROS BUNKER
From air raid shelter to art world sanctuary

On the corner of Reinhardstraße and Albrechtstraße in Mitte there is a five-storey square monolith with 1.8-metre- (6-foot-) thick reinforced concrete walls and a 3-metre- (10-foot-) thick flat roof. It is quite elegant as bunkers go and was completed in 1942 as the Reichsbahnbunker Friedrichstraße, providing shelter from air raids for up to 3,000 passengers using the nearby train station. The building was designed by Karl Bonatz (1882–1951) under the supervision of Albert Speer (1905–81), Hitler's chief architect.

After the war, it was used variously as a textile and fruit and veg warehouse until the 1990s, when its labyrinthine interior of 161 rooms hosted a claustrophobic hardcore techno club where sweat literally ran down the walls. The structure was also used as a temporary exhibition space around this time, which must have caught the eye of art collector Christian Boros, who bought it in 2003 to house both his family and his impressive contemporary art collection. Boros charged Berlin firm Realarchitektur to burrow out some 3,000 square metres (3,230 square feet) of exhibition space and add a 500 square-metre (5,381 square-foot) roof-level extension, a stunning glass-walled, Mies-like apartment complete with chainmail-curtain sunshades and a lap pool.

Known today as the Boros Bunker, this massive structure now houses works from artists including Olafur Eliasson, Sarah Lucas, Rirkrit Tiravanija, Ai Weiwei, Wolfgang Tillmans and Alicja Kwade. Viewing is by appointment only.

# BIER BEER
A no logo enterprise

Like it says on the label, this is a beer called 'beer' – no need to bother remembering the brand. Already a staple in Berlin bars and at gallery openings, Bier Bier is as about as new Berlinish as you can get.

It is what it says on the bottle: beer. Bier Bier is one of many small, new, independent beverage labels that have sprung up around the city in recent years.

Founded in Berlin in 2009 by two friends, Johannes Schwaderer and Stephan Alutis, Bier Bier combines a minimalistic label design with the idea of a straightforward product. With the initial success of their brewed beverage, the small company has in the last years expanded their product line to include equally straightforward cola and *Weinschorle* (wine spritzer). The very absence of a loud logo makes this range of beverages stand out against the rest. 'The goal of this project is to take a stand against the visual pollution to which people in urban environments are constantly subjected' say the founders, taking their cue from German designer Dieter Rams' Ten Principles of Design, one of which states: 'Good design is as little design as possible'.

German beer adheres to the traditional 16th-century *Reinheitsgebot* (German Beer Purity Law), which rules that beer may only be brewed using barley, hops and water – nothing else – and the Germans take it very seriously. Beer is, after all, classified as an essential foodstuff in this country.

**BIER**

0,33l

# PRINZESSINNENGÄRTEN
Urban gardening at its best

The Prinzessinengärten (Princess Gardens) are neither the first nor last urban gardening project in Berlin, yet they can be seen as a symbol for many. A grassroots initiative (in the most literal sense), they were founded by the non-profit organization Nomadisch Grün as an experimental pilot project in 2009 on a Kreuzberg site that had been an urban wasteland for over half a century. Volunteers joined together to clear away rubbish, build containers for plants and vegetables and soon reaped the first fruits of their labours. The DIY aesthetic of the entire place – from the container café at the back to the constructions of recycled wood everywhere and the 'as found' furniture – may appear to scream 'Berlin hipster', but this is more than just hipsterism. It is the realisation of a dream to create 'urban culture' by bringing people of many different backgrounds together in this very multi-culti district. The project works surprisingly well in this location, beside a busy city roundabout.

The Prinzessinengärten are completely open to the public with free entrance to all. Anyone can join in the gardening efforts and participate in the offered activities – from bar and garden café to many different cultural events and workshops. The gardens attract a very diverse audience of locals and tourists as well as the international hipster crowd – unavoidable in Berlin today. Big plus: the food is really yummy!

From squats and graffiti to clubs and informal play spaces or vegetable gardens: Berliners are masters at reclaiming urban spaces in the name of the 'urban commons'.

# AUGUSTSTRASSE
Art, architecture and auras

Every street in Berlin bears the marks of history, but few have quite so many layers of scars and ornamentations as Auguststraße in Mitte. It is also a model street for where the post-Wall gentrification of the city took hold. Auguststraße gained its name and many of its buildings in the mid-19th century only to have half of them knocked out like so many teeth in the Second World War. In the 1990s, many artists moved into its run-down unmodernized buildings and built the beginnings of the early post-unification gallery scene. The most prominent of them is the Kunst-Werke at number 69, a former margarine factory that was occupied by squatters in the 1990s and is now a stalwart of the contemporary art scene.

Although nearly all the gaps between the buildings are now filled and much has been renovated, there are still shocking reminders of the past. Auguststraße was at the heart of Berlin's Jewish community from the mid-19th century until the early 1930s. The former Jewish Girls' School at number 11, a Neue Sachlichkeit-style (New Objectivity-style) building from 1930, served its purpose for just three years before being closed. Most of its former students and teachers were deported and murdered by the Nazis. After a fairly sensitive renovation by Berlin-based Grüntuch-Ernst Architects in 2012, it now houses a Michelin-starred restaurant, galleries, a deli and a bar, but its history can make it an uncomfortable place to be.

Down the road at number 24 is the still bullet-ridden and carefully preserved decaying façade of Clärchens Ballhaus, a traditional dance hall built in 1913 that is – astoundingly – still going strong over a century later. Amid foxtrotting couples and laughing diners and drinkers on a winter's evening, one feels here that time has not so much stood still as exists all at once, folded together in the layers of the building's fabric.

An architectural melting pot that's as much contemporary cultural barometer as it is a history lesson: it doesn't get much more Berlin than Auguststraße (below). The Spiegelsaal (Hall of Mirrors) in Clärchens Ballhaus (opposite) can be hired for private events.

# POTSDAMER STRASSE 77–87
On gentrification and reappropriation

You won't find Potsdamer Straße 77–87 in any architecture guide. The lot is entered through a driveway between the – mainly 1950s – front houses which leads to a roughly paved, semi-carpark at the back with a cluster of remaining *Altbauten* (old buildings) from the 19th century and a former German Electricity Union building from 1912, which housed the Berlin broadsheet *Der Tagesspiegel* between 1954 and 2009.

Potsdamer Straße is home to both the sweeping exhibition spaces of the private Blain|Southern gallery (top) and Andreas Murkudis (below), Berlin's best-curated concept store, which is world-renowned in fashion circles.

No icons here, one would think, but what is iconic about it is what it represents: Berlin as the capital of adaptation, reappropriation, evolution and change. Like several other high streets in Berlin, such as Torstraße in Mitte, post-Wall Potsdamer Straße was a failing, shabby street whose only highlights were the Wintergarten variety theatre (at number 96), the Victoria Bar's (number 102) cocktails and the handful of aging hookers, left over from its days as a West Berlin red-light district, on the street corners. Now, in the space of a few short years, it has been struck by the process of change known as 'gentrification' and the pioneers, as ever, are the art galleries and related businesses.

At number 77–87, among other newish arrivals, you will find the expensively swish Blain|Southern gallery next to Galerie Thomas Fischer's much more modest, but no less intriguing premises. Here too is Andreas Murkudis' beautifully reduced concept store, legendary among refined fashionistas worldwide and, above him, in the former *Tagesspiegel* tower are the offices and showrooms of the furniture company Artek.

# KLUNKERKRANICH
A community playground for grown-ups

To call the Klunkerkranich (wattled crane), established in 2013, a design icon may seem a bit premature. But besides being a perfect location for a sundowner, this rooftop bar in the middle of hip Neukölln is a wonderful example of the kind of bar/club Berlin is so beloved for. On top of a shopping-centre car park a group of friends, who are also behind the club Fuchs und Elster, succeeded in creating this attractive green oasis, where art, nightlife, and community are merged into a very agreeable experience.

Most Berliners are familiar with the aesthetic: like many other legendary nightclubs, most notably the now defunct Bar 25, the Klunkerkranich has an improvised, DIY, wooden adventure playground-style aesthetic, incorporating a range of diversions which make it essentially a playground for grown-ups.

But the Klunkerkranich is also more than just a bar or club, its aim is to provide an alternative to the concrete jungle for everyone in the local community, not just night owls dancing to techno music. It may be a great place to enjoy a sunset over Neukölln tapping into the free wifi with your mobile office, but it is also open day and night, offering breakfast, gardening workshops, lectures and children's programmes – drawing in the local community, shoppers and clubbers alike to meet, participate and get involved.

The Klunkerkranich, or wattled crane, is an endangered species, and so too are many of the improvised initiatives, clubs, bars, galleries and art projects that have made this city such a magnet for visitors from abroad. They represent another kind of community-based development that no amount of real-estate investment money can buy.

# STADTBAD MITTE
Public leisure and architectural pleasure

London has its lidos, Paris its *piscines* and Berlin has its *Bäder* – a rich medley of architecturally delightful swimming pools, both outdoor and in, ranging from neoclassical bathhouses like the Stadtbad Neukölln via 1930s lakeside lidos complete with beach (Stadtbad Wannsee) to state-of-the-art Olympic-sized complexes like the one on Landsbergerallee in Prenzlauer Berg.

One of my favourite places to take a dive is Stadtbad Mitte in Gartenstraße. This elegantly functional pool was designed in the late 1920s when public swimming and bathing facilities were built as much for public health as they were for leisure. In an era when light, sun and air were considered paramount for hygiene, architect Carlo Jelkmann installed stunning ribbon windows across the walls and ceilings, allowing daylight to pour into the cavernous hall above the pool.

The interior design of the structure was overseen by Heinrich Tessenow (1876–1950), a contemporary of Bruno Taut and Hans Poelzig and one of the most important architects of the Weimar era. His scheme for the large and complex layout included fine detailing from ochre wall tiles to bronze and frosted glass entrance-hall lamps in keeping with his working motto: 'The simplest form is not always the best, but the best is always simple.'

The well-renovated splendour of the Stadtbad Mitte. There are some amazing indoor and outdoor swimming pools in Berlin, and others worth a visit include the Sommerbad Olympiastadion, the Olympic-sized Schwimm- und Sprunghalle at Landsberger Allee, the romanesque Stadtbad Neukölln and the penthouse pool with a view at the Hyatt Hotel.

# TEMPELHOF AIRPORT SKATE PARK
Kickflipping history

One of Berlin's most extraordinary public spaces is the former Tempelhof airfield that once hosted the Western Allies' deliveries of fuel and food during the 11-month Soviet blockade of the city after the Second World War. This enormous field, complete with runway, is now a haven for kite fliers, barbecuers, urban gardeners, promenaders and, in particular, skateboarders.

1000 Plateaus, as it is officially known, is not technically a skate park but rather a piece of 'urban sculpture' by architect John Lang, situated beside the former runway. The stone covering the 1,500-square- metre (16,000-square- foot) area is just some of the vast quantity of granite recycled from the Palast der Republik in Mitte. This GDR parliament building-cum-entertainment complex designed by Heinz Graffunder (1926–94) and Karl-Ernst Swora (1933–2001) in 1976 was deemed unfit for purpose during the 1990s and therefore (somewhat controversially) demolished and recycled in 2008.

The Tempelhofer Feld skate park was built with the help of teenage volunteers and is the brainchild of skater Adam Sello. It is one of the many artistic and horticultural social-use projects that can be found scattered across the former airfield. Combining the flotsam of 20th-century history with self-initiated resourcefulness, this is upcycling, Berlin-style. A more than fitting approach for the city famously damned by critic Karl Scheffler in 1920 as 'always becoming and never to be'.

The inner-city Tempelhof airport finally closed for business in 2008. Since then its runways have been taken over by the citizens and its vast building (one of the largest in Europe) currently houses both events and refugees. When property developers hoped to grab some of the land for new building projects, thousands of Berliners blocked the move with a petition and a referendum.

# INDEX

# PICTURE CREDITS

# CREDITS

An Hachette UK Company
www.hachette.co.uk

First published in
Great Britain in 2017
by Conran Octopus,
a division of Octopus
Publishing Group Ltd,
in conjunction with
the Design Museum

Octopus Publishing
Group Ltd
Carmelite House
50 Victoria Embankment
London EC4Y 0DZ
www.octopusbooks.co.uk
www.octopusbooksusa.com

Distributed in the US by
Hachette Book Group
1290 Avenue of the
Americas, 4th and 5th Floors,
New York, NY 10020

Distributed in Canada by
Canadian Manda Group
664 Annette St., Toronto,
Ontario, Canada  M6S 2C8

Sophie Lovell asserts the
moral right to be identified as
the author of this work.

A CIP catalogue record for
this book is available from the
British Library.

*Text written by:*
Sophie Lovell

*Commissioning Editor:*
Joe Cottington
*Consultant Editor:*
Deyan Sudjic
*Senior Editor:*
Alex Stetter
*Additional text and research:*
Florian Heilmeyer,
George Kafka, Sebastian
Schumacher, Fiona
Shipwright, Rob Wilson,
&beyond collective
*Copy Editor:*
Jane Birch
*Design:*
Untitled
*Picture Research Manager:*
Giulia Hetherington
*Picture Researcher:*
Sophie Hartley
*Production Controller:*
Dasha Miller

Based on a concept by
Hugh Devlin

Printed and bound in China

ISBN 978 1 84091 741 3

10 9 8 7 6 5 4 3 2 1

The Design Museum is one of the world's leading museums of contemporary design. Design Museum Members enjoy free unlimited entry to the museum's outstanding exhibitions as well as access to events, tours and discounts. Becoming a Member is an inspiring way to support the museum's work. Visit designmuseum.org/become-a-member and get involved today.